EAT LIKE A LOCAL- ECUADOR

Ecuador Food Guide

Martina Miño Pérez

Eat Like a Local-Equador Copyright © 2019 by CZYK Publishing LLC. All Rights Reserved.

All rights reserved. No part of this book may be reproduced in any form or by any electronic or mechanical means including information storage and retrieval systems, without permission in writing from the author. The only exception is by a reviewer, who may quote short excerpts in a review.

The statements in this book are of the authors and may not be the views of CZYK Publishing.

Cover designed by: Lisa Rusczyk Ed. D.

CZYK
PUBLISHING

CZYK Publishing Since 2011.

Eat Like a Local

Lock Haven, PA
All rights reserved.
ISBN: 9798607903664

BOOK DESCRIPTION

Are you excited about planning your next trip?

Do you want an edible experience? Would you like some culinary guidance from a local? If you answered yes to any of these questions, then this Eat Like a Local book is for you. Eat Like a Local, Ecuador by Author Martina Miño Pérez presents new insight on Ecuadorian gastronomy and its diverse culinary identities. Culinary tourism is an important aspect of any travel experience. Food has the ability to tell you a story of a destination, its landscapes, and culture on a single plate. Most food guides tell you how to eat like a tourist. Although there is nothing wrong with that, as part of the Eat Like a Local series, this book will give you a food guide from someone who has lived at your next culinary destination.

In these pages, you will discover advice on having a unique edible experience. This book will not tell you exact addresses or hours but instead will give you excitement and knowledge of food and drinks from a local that you may not find in other travel food guides.

Eat like a local. Slow down, stay in one place, and get to know the food, people, and culture. By the time you finish this book, you will be eager and prepared to travel to your next culinary destination.

OUR STORY

Traveling has always been a passion of the creator of the Eat Like a Local book series. During Lisa's travels in Malta, instead of tasting what the city offered, she ate at a large fast-food chain. However, she realized that her traveling experience would have been more fulfilling if she had experienced the best of local cuisines. Most would agree that food is one of the most important aspects of a culture. Through her travels, Lisa learned how much locals had to share with tourists, especially about food. Lisa created the Eat Like a Local book series to help connect people with locals which she discovered is a topic that locals are very passionate about sharing. So please join me and: Eat, drink, and explore like a local.

TABLE OF CONTENTS

BOOK DESCRIPTION
OUR STORY
TABLE OF CONTENTS
DEDICATION
ABOUT THE AUTHOR
HOW TO USE THIS BOOK
FROM THE PUBLISHER

1. Prepare your Stomach for an Amazing Culinary Journey.
2. Life in the Altitude: Arriving to Quito.
3. Don't Let Altitude Sickness Stop You! Get Your Coca Leaves!
4. Ecuadorian Gastronomy and its "Mestizaje".
5. The Andes are Full of Edible Treasures.
6. If there is a Heaven, It Would be Full of Empanadas.
7. Hooked on Yam Bread.
8. Huecas: The Hidden Gold Mines of Taste.
9. Eating at the Market: A Multi-Sensorial Experience.
10. Fruits in All their Forms.
11. Ají will Make Every Meal Better!
12. The Rumors are True. We Eat Guinea Pigs.
13. Steamed Corn Delicacies.

14. Quito Can Get Cold, Luckily we Have Great Soups.
15. Upholding Ecuadorian Gastronomy.
16. Street Food is the Gastronomic Soul of Every City.
17. The Boom of Craft Beer.
18. Chicha is How we Roll.
19. Achachay, it's Cold! Bring Canelazo!
20. Blue Bird.
21. Ecuadorian Food is Quite Meat-Based. What if I am Vegetarian?
22. Ok, There is Great Food in Quito, How do I Pay for It?
23. Another Tricky Question: How Much Will I Pay for my Food?
24. Ambato is the Land of Fruits and Flowers.
25. Holy Water Baths.
26. Craft Markets in Otavalo.
27. Cotopaxi Volcano: The Neck of the Moon.
28. The Avenue of the Volcanoes.
29. Cuenca: A Cultural and Gastronomic Gem.
30. Reserva Natural El Cajas: A Gift from the Ice Age.
31. Enjoying a meal in the Cloudy Forest.
32. How About Some Worms?
33. Eating from the Rainforest.

34. The Red Seed.
35. Cacao is our Gold.
36. Coffee is Also Our Gold!
37. Cooking with Leaves.
38. Cooking with Mud.
39. Ceviche is Life!
40. Welcome to Manabí! Ready to Eat?
41. A Gustative Re-Birth.
42. The Three Kinds of Milk of the Coconut.
43. G-KILL CITY. The Home of the Best Encebollado.
44. The Galapagos Islands: Where to Eat on a Fragile Paradise?
45. During Easter, we Eat Fanesca!
46. Christmas in the Tropics. Really?
47. Burning the Old and Building the New.
48. The Day of the Dead.
49. I'm tired of Ecuadorian Food, is There Something Else?
50. Chau Ecuador! What Flavours will I Take with Me?

Other resources:

READ OTHER BOOKS BY CZYK PUBLISHING

DEDICATION

I dedicate this book to my partner, Sébastien. He is not only the best cooking mate, but also the person that reminds me how important is to remain curious, cook new dishes, and taste unexpected flavors. Every time we cook together I remember how essential food is in life and how much happiness it can bring.

ABOUT THE AUTHOR

Martina is an artist, writer and cook born in Ecuador. She currently lives, works, and cooks between Berlin, Helsinki and Quito. Martina just graduated from her Masters in Visual Culture, Curating and Contemporary Art at Aalto University, where she researched the relationship between eating, cooking, and philosophical thinking. Her thesis: "Cooking and Eating as Metaphorical Thinking" was published in Finland in June. In 2018 she also published her first cookbook called Cooking from Memory where she presented ice cream recipes connected to specific memories. This book was part of her exhibition Memory Popsicles: An Exhibition of Edible Pasts, which took part in Helsinki Design Week.

Martina loves to cook but more than anything else, she loves to reflect upon food; it's philosophical and poetic aspects and how eating can lead us to absorb and digest new knowledge. She hopes to continue working on her edible artworks around the world and find new ways in which food can communicate meaning.

Besides working as a freelancer, cooking and making art, Martina enjoys reading in public transportation, writing poetry in the bathroom, and listening to her collection of records on repeat.

HOW TO USE THIS BOOK

The goal of this book is to help culinary travelers either dream or experience different edible experiences by providing opinions from a local. The author has made suggestions based on their own knowledge. Please do your own research before traveling to the area in case the suggested locations are unavailable.

Travel Advisories: As a first step in planning any trip abroad, check the Travel Advisories for your intended destination.
https://travel.state.gov/content/travel/en/traveladvisories/traveladvisories.html

FROM THE PUBLISHER

Traveling can be one of the most important parts of a person's life. The anticipation and memories that you have are some of the best. As a publisher of the *Eat Like a Local*, Greater Than a Tourist, as well as the popular *50 Things to Know* book series, we strive to help you learn about new places, spark your imagination, and inspire you. Wherever you are and whatever you do I wish you safe, fun, and inspiring travel.

Lisa Rusczyk Ed. D.
CZYK Publishing

Eat Like a Local

"Ecuadorians are strange and unique beings: they sleep peacefully surrounded by roaring volcanoes, they live poorly among incomparable richness and become happy listening to sad music"

- Alexander Von Humboldt.

Bienvenidos y bienvenidas to Ecuador!

It's great you are considering travelling to Ecuador for your next trip! Maybe you've heard it's crossed by the equatorial line and that it is seen as the "centre of the world". All of this is true! Nevertheless, I think it's worth saying: Ecuador is much, much more than an imaginary line. I emphasize this, as countless times people have asked me: "So, on what part of the line do you live?" Ayayay! Please skip this question.

More than a guide to the most touristic places in Ecuador, this guide will lead you to the hidden gastronomic treasures of the country and show you how to get to them. Think of it as a treasure map! In

Ecuador, you will encounter mind-blowing landscapes, unique flora and fauna, great hikes, and friendly people, but also amazing food that you might not be able to taste anywhere else in the world. Before guiding you into this gastronomic journey, let me start by giving you a visual image of the place you are about to visit. Ecuador is one of the smallest countries in South America, yet one of the most biodiverse in the world. The country is divided in four regions: The Andes, the Amazon, the Coast, and the Galapagos Islands. Ecuador is not only diverse in its flora and fauna but also in the various forms of cooking that exist around the country. Each region doesn't only contain different cultural identities but also various layers of culinary heritage. This makes Ecuadorian food an open book of gustatory history, where every recipe and ingredient says something important about its national identities.

     Ecuador is a hidden gem of great depth and complexity. At every corner, the landscape will change; from the altitude of the Andes and the Cloudy Forests to the richness of the Amazon and vastness of the Pacific Ocean. This country will show you an aspect of South America you've never seen before, so in order to enjoy this experience to the

Eat Like a Local

fullest, travel with an open mind and with curiosity to taste new things.

Through this guide, I will share with you some practical tips, from how to keep your stomach healthy, how to deal with altitude sickness, where to find the best places to eat in each city, to the most interesting ingredients from each region. ¡QUÉ DISFRUTEN!

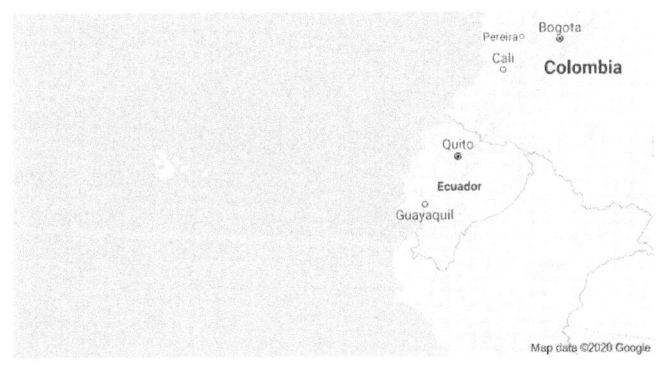

Ecuador

Eat Like a Local

Quito Ecuador Climate

	High	Low
January	66	49
February	66	49
March	66	49
April	66	49
May	66	49
June	67	48
July	67	47
August	68	48
September	68	47
October	67	48
November	67	48
December	66	48

GreaterThanaTourist.com

Temperatures are in Fahrenheit degrees.
Source: NOAA

1. PREPARE YOUR STOMACH FOR AN AMAZING CULINARY JOURNEY.

Food is such an important part of a trip; and, if you consider yourself to be what we call "buen diente" or a foodie, it is important you bring a healthy and happy stomach along. When visiting Ecuador, many of my friends and my boyfriend have had stomach issues during their first days in the country. In every part of the world, bacteria found in food and water are different and your stomach might feel a bit shocked and unsettled with the new coming guests. You can diminish the possible discomfort of this adaptation process by drinking some probiotics before your trip and improving your general intestinal flora as much as possible. Once in the country, keep in mind to always drink bottled or boiled water. Don't drink tap water and try to avoid raw vegetables that might have been washed with it. Many people say it is safe to drink tap water, at least in Quito, however, the condition of some pipes is often poor and this might affect the ultimate quality of the water. After you spend a couple of weeks in the country you can count on your stomach feeling stronger and more prepared to process bacteria from tap water. Then you can enjoy some fresh salads, juices and fresh sauces!

2. LIFE IN THE ALTITUDE: ARRIVING TO QUITO.

Whether you arrive in Quito by airplane, bus, or car, you will find that the city is geographically stunning. Caray! Quito lies at an altitude of 2,850 meters above sea level and it is the second-highest capital in the world. It stretches through an inter-Andean valley between two mountain ranges and many volcanoes surround it. Some of them are deep asleep, while others are very much active. On a clear day, you might be lucky enough to see the snowy peaks of Cotopaxi, Cayambe, and Antisana from pretty much anywhere in the city.

Quito, as a very elevated metropolis, brings you closer to the sun. Considering you will be in the equator, it might come to your attention that at midday your body will cast no shadow. As cool as this might sound, be very careful with the sun. Be sure to wear sunblock every day, even if it's cloudy or rainy. The U.V. rays in the equatorial region are very high and at this altitude even more. So take care of your skin and enjoy the lovely heat from the sun! This brings me to the second important point concerning your arrival. Once you arrive, it will be very likely you will suffer from altitude sickness or what we call soroche. Don't worry, there is nothing life-threatening about it, this only means that your body will take some time to adapt to a higher altitude. You might feel your heart pumping faster, and maybe you will be tired for the first few days. Don't push it, give your body some time and rest to acclimate.

People respond differently to altitude. While some might suffer from prolonged symptoms, others might barely feel anything. If you belong to the first group, the next chapter will introduce some of the approaches people use to acclimate to Andean grounds.

3. DON'T LET ALTITUDE SICKNESS STOP YOU! GET YOUR COCA LEAVES!

Soroche can be unpleasant, and everyone, even Quiteños suffer from it when returning from lower lands to altitude, no matter how many years they have lived in the highlands. Fortunately, it is only temporary, and there are ways to diminish its symptoms. In the whole Andean region, the practice of chewing Coca leaves is one of the oldest (dating back 8000 years) and most effective remedies for altitude sickness. Let me remark that the consumption of Coca leaves proposed in this text has nothing to do with the drug cocaine, and that it is a safe, legal and natural alternative to help with your altitude sickness. You can buy Coca leaves as tea bags from any pharmacy or organic food store and drink it as an infusion. You can also buy it in the form of candy and enjoy its herbal taste as you hike through the magnificent Andean landscapes. No secondary effects, just pure healing magic that will bring your body back to life! Additionally, to help even more with altitude sickness it is recommended to eat light during the first days of your visit and avoid dishes rich in fat.

4. ECUADORIAN GASTRONOMY AND ITS "MESTIZAJE".

Before we start drooling and immersing into the world of flavours, let us go through some reflections upon why Ecuadorian food is the way it is. Ecuadorians have a very mixed and complex combination of identities and heritage. From ethnic groups such as Mestizos (Spanish & Indigenous) and Mulatos (Spanish & Afro-Descendant) to Indigenous, Cholos, Montubios, Afro-Ecuadorian, Arab, Jewish, Indian, Chinese and even Jamaican; our genealogies are diverse and beautiful. In the case of the indigenous ethnic groups of Ecuador, they each possess their own language, customs, and culture. Imagine how they all enrich our gastronomy! Ecuadorian food is a blend of different culinary traditions, ingredients, and cooking techniques. Many plates from the highlands, for example, combine the culinary traditions of Spanish cuisine with the ingredients of pre-hispanic cooking in the Andes. In the coast, in provinces such as Esmeraldas, Manabí and El Guayas, the food reflects the ingredients used by the Afro-Ecuadorian communities. Coconut milk, fish, rice, green banana, coriander, lime juice, and fresh seafood are a must when preparing a successful plato costeño. Each region in Ecuador has gone through a different type of cultural mix, which is represented through the food people cook, the ingredients they use, and how they name their dishes.

5. THE ANDES ARE FULL OF EDIBLE TREASURES.

If your first destination in Ecuador is Quito and the Andean region, be prepared to discover the delicious treasures that grow under its soils and on top of them. Potato and corn are native to the Andean region, therefore they are an essential part of the Ecuadorian diet. We use their countless varieties in our most typical dishes. From soups such as Locro de Papas to fried patties filled with cheese like Llapingachos, potatoes are a huge part of our gastronomic heritage. Our most important traditional dishes will contain them! Corn, unlike México, is not used to making the dough for tortillas but is the basic ingredient of dishes like Empanadas de Morocho, Sopa de Morocho (a type of corn soup), and aromatic drinks like Rosero (juice made with corn, anis, lemon verbena, and strawberries). Ecuadorians also enjoy eating corn al natural by boiling it and then topping it with some salt, butter, fresh cheese and some hot sauce on the side. Potatoes and corn are the base of our pre-hispanic cuisine and when cooked correctly they become sublime. Rice is also a winner side dish through the whole country. I personally love to eat the Cocolón or roasted leftovers of rice that remain at the bottom of the casserole, deliciously crunchy and smoked.

6. IF THERE IS A HEAVEN, IT WOULD BE FULL OF EMPANADAS.

Do you enjoy eating dumplings? Does your mouth water when thinking about Calzone? Well, my mouth drools when I think of eating an Empanada. Just thinking of its crunchy outside dough and its juicy filling makes me emotional. In Ecuador, there are several varieties of this dish, their ingredients and filling vary depending on where they are made. Empanada de Morocho, for example, is one of the cheapest and most delicious types of street food you will find in Quito and in many other Andean towns. Its crunchy outside made of Morocho (a type of white corn) protects a juicy inside of carrots, peas, grounded meat and cumin. This salty snack is always sided with Ají, our national hot sauce. Similarly, Empanada de Viento is known for being a street delicacy, yet, its filing is mostly air... and some salty cheese. The great thing about this Empanada is that it's huge, and through the frying process, it swells like a balloon. Don't forget to top it with some white sugar and eat it with your hands!

Empanadas are a national dish, and if you travel to the coast you will encounter one of the most venerated varieties of that region: La Empanada de Verde. Its name describes the use of green banana as the main ingredient for its dough. This Empanada is commonly filled with cheese or shrimp and then deep-fried, of course. Don't forget to eat it with some Ají! Wherever you are in the country, Empanadas will not be hard to find, and you don't have to look for them, they will find you. However, in case you want to find the best Empanadas in Quito, you could go to Las Tripas de la Floresta, an ambulant eating court that becomes alive every evening in the neighbourhood of La Floresta. If your budget is a little bit higher, you can get a delicate assortment of

Eat Like a Local

amazing empanadas in Hotel Casa Gangotena. You will not regret paying some extra dollars for this experience. In case you want to take your Empanada experience to another level, I suggest you bite off the top, pour a generous amount of Ají inside it, and eat it with your hands. DELICIOSO!

7. HOOKED ON YAM BREAD.

The same way Ecuadorians are obsessed with Empanadas, they are equally hooked with Pan de Yuca or yam bread. This cheesy, crunchy, and mouth-watering snack is cooked with tapioca or yam starch, cheese, eggs, and butter. It sounds very simple, but you will be surprised by its texture. It is gooey and cheesy on the inside, yet crunchy on its outside. This dish is so popular, that you will find people selling it on buses and on the street, baking it on a mini oven on the side of the road. This is a type of bread that is especially popular on the coast and people eat it together with a glass of fruit yoghurt. Yes, that sounds strange, but wait until you try it. I've seen many foreigners becoming really obsessed with this snack. My boyfriend, for example, is now creating his own version of Pan de Yuca, filling it with some french cheese or aromatizing it with thyme. You can find this cheesy delicacy in most bakeries in Quito, however, Yogurt Amazonas and the cafeteria Cassave, are places specialized in cooking this local snack.

8. HUECAS: THE HIDDEN GOLD MINES OF TASTE.

If you ask me, the greatest Ecuadorian food is cooked by my grandmother, but assuming you will not bump into her, I suggest you visit some Huecas. These informal and popular low-budget restaurants, also known as agachaditos offer the real deal! Here you will have the best Ecuadorian food experiences. Ecuador is full of Huecas and informal restaurants; nevertheless, it is important that by word of mouth you reach the best ones. There are many Ecuadorian recipes that are slowly disappearing from the gastronomic radar but that, fortunately, can still be found in the Huecas. In Quito, delicacies such as Tripa Mishki (intestines with peanut sauce and potato), Hornado (slow-cooked pork), Empanadas, and Choclo con Queso (corn with fresh cheese), are some of the popular dishes among locals. Some of my favourite Huecas in Quito are El Ville de la Ciudadela León, where you will taste a unique veal broth, which is famous for improving "fertility", Los Encebollados de las Cinco Esquinas, a classic Hueca that serves the best fish soup to cure even the worst hangover, and the Sandwiches of La Plaza Grande, the best cured pork sandwiches in the Historical Center. Besides these, don't miss out on other unique agachaditos such as Las Guatitas de la Colmena; Los Canelazos de la Ronda; Los Motes de San Juan; Las Corvinas de Gloria; and the delicious Morocho drink from Morochos Tradicionalmente Quiteños.

9. EATING AT THE MARKET: A MULTI-SENSORIAL EXPERIENCE.

Markets are the best places to try new local flavours and I love to visit them because of their colour, their smell, their energy and their people. I also prefer to buy from the market, rather than from supermarkets, to support local producers. In Ecuador, there is still a strong tradition of cooking homemade remedies using herbs, and markets offer unique plants with amazing properties. Besides herbs, fruits and vegetables, and the spice corners, most markets also have a food court. If you visit Mercado Iñaquito in the North of Quito, don't forget to enjoy a plate of Hornado. This dish includes a slow-cooked and tender piece of pork meat, accompanied with a spoon of corn (mote), a portion of sweet-sour encebollado made of red onion, lime juice and tomato, and a pair of Llapingachos. If you eat this plate for lunch, don't worry about dinner, you will be full for the rest of the day.

If you prefer fish, you can't miss out on the Corvinas del Mercado San Roque. This market located in the historical centre will offer you the best piece of fish you can try in the city. Accompanied by a bowl of shrimp and oyster ceviche, this deep-fried filet of sea bass will never leave your mind. Now, if you are feeling adventurous and wish to try something out of the ordinary, you might be interested in trying Yaguarlocro in the Mercado de la Magdalena. This popular dish is basically a Locro, our local potato soup, cooked with milk, peanuts, tripe, intestine, and aromatic touch of oregano. To take it one step further, this potage is topped with pieces of fried blood (yaguar in Quechua). As strange as this might sound, it is very tasty and a perfect soup for a "winter" day in Quito.

Last but not least, the JUICE STANDS. Every market in the country has at least one juice stand and you will know where it is by the orchestral sound of its eight blenders on the counter. The smell of fresh fruit will also be a good guide for you to get there. Juice stands don't only offer a great variety and generous glasses of fresh fruit juice but also sell exotic blends with egg yolk, herbs and spices, for specific medicinal purposes. By the way, fruit juice is an indispensable beverage that must be included in every Ecuadorian meal. So if you love smoothies, and you feel you are able to drink them as often as three times a day, you are in the right place!

10. FRUITS IN ALL THEIR FORMS.

As you already know, fruit juice is a big deal in Ecuador and I can dare to say that it is enjoyed by a huge majority of the population, if not all of it. Fruit in Ecuador is abundant, varied and accessible. Only by walking around the city you will encounter fruit trees on your way, some offering fresh lemon, and others naranja agria, our local type of bitter orange. In Ecuador fruit is an indispensable part of people's diets. My mother, for example, can't start her morning without eating a fresh piece of papaya. The prices for most fruits are low and many of them grow all year round. Furthermore, the different types of microclimates particular to each region of the country offer unique types of fruit you will only find there. Naranjilla, Taxo, Guanábana, Guaba, Tuna, Pitajaya, Uvilla, and Capulí are just some examples of the fruit paradise you will encounter on arrival. There is no English translation for many of these fruits, so you should write their names down and ask for them in the market.

Eat Like a Local

11. AJÍ WILL MAKE EVERY MEAL BETTER!

Ají is the "official" hot sauce of Ecuador. I might be wrong, but I have never met a single Ecuadorian who doesn't enjoy some ají on their rice. Its name comes from the type of pepper we use, red, medium-size and subtle in taste. Ají is a sauce that is not meant to be overpowering with spiciness, but that is fresh and aromatic. During your journey through Ecuador, you will encounter different types of Ají, and you will love them all. In the highlands, Ají sauce is made using a fruit called Tomate de árbol (tree tomato), which is a bit sour, therefore it is not eaten raw but made into juices, jams and sauces. Tomate de árbol makes Ají fruity and thick. Its texture is great to top any soup, stew or even plain potatoes. In the coast, Ají is less thick and more acid. By using vinegar and small-diced vegetables like carrots, this type of Ají comes to be closer to a pickled sauce. It's sharp and salty taste breaks through the richness of seafood and brings contrast to the dish. Personally, my favorite variation of this sauce is Ají de Maní, which has a base of peanut blended with milk and coriander. Its texture is creamy and smooth.

12. THE RUMORS ARE TRUE. WE EAT GUINEA PIGS.

It was in the summer of 2010, during a visit to Montpellier when I met for the first time a Guinea Pig that was someone's pet. It lived the life of a king, and as it crawled into its owner's arms, I remember thinking it was very cute. Before this, I had never seen any Guinea Pig, or Cuy as we call it in Ecuador, actually alive. I had just seen them roasting on a stick on the side of the road in the town of Sangolquí. Surprisingly, their smell can follow you for several kilometers and impregnates on your clothes. Cuy is an emblematic dish across the Andes; nevertheless, it produces strong reactions on people. Some people love it, some people hate it, and they can't ever seem to agree. As a gastronomic experience, it is interesting to try this dish, and reach your own conclusions. In the town of Selva Alegre, picanterías such as Gabrielita and El Hueco serve delicious Cuy sided with potatoes, peanut sauce, tomato slices and lettuce. If you travel by car through the Ecuadorian highlands you will find places where to eat this delicacy everywhere. You better put your seatbelt on!

Eat Like a Local

13. STEAMED CORN DELICACIES.

You might be wondering, why is corn so important for Ecuadorians? Well, besides its versatility and amazing taste, corn is an ancestral ingredient that during the Inca Empire was considered a sacred symbol of abundance and fertility. It formed part of funerary and religious ceremonies and was an important element in the sacrifices to mother earth when asking for rain in times of drought. Corn is our Andean gold and dishes such as Tamales and Humitas exemplify this. In the case of my family, we eat these on special occasions like birthdays or graduations and we pair them with a nice cup of cinnamon tea. Tamales and Humitas are steamed puddings or loaves of corn wrapped into Achira leaves or corn leaves. While Tamal can contain other ingredients in its dough such as olives, paprika, egg and some shredded chicken, Humita is plain, and we enjoy eating it with a slice of melted butter on top. Both of them are delicious and you will be able to find them in practically any cafeteria in Quito or other towns in the Ecuadorian highlands. Commonly we eat them at tea time, as a merienda in the company of friends and family, or by ourselves in the company of a good book.

14. QUITO CAN GET COLD, LUCKILY WE HAVE GREAT SOUPS.

Let me make something clear. Quito is a city that can get REALLY COLD at night, especially during its rainy season. Yes, you will be in the Equator, which is "closer to the sun", however, the temperatures change drastically throughout the day. So be prepared to take some clothes for spring, summer and winter in your luggage. During the rainy season in Quito, which commonly starts around October, the sun still offers its pleasant heat in the mornings, nevertheless, this can change in the lapse of an hour, giving room to a massive tempest in the afternoon. In the highlands, you will notice a thick layer of neblina or fog arriving from the South and filling up the whole city in a mist. When this happens, you will know it is quite cold, probably seven or eight degrees. Ecuadorian houses don't have heating, so that's great, it will be cold inside the house too.

Eat Like a Local

Luckily, there are great hot soups that will make you forget even the meaning of coldness.

Ecuadorians have a strong tradition of soups, from a good old Caldo de Gallina (our version of chicken soup) to a Timbushka (meat broth with potato, cabbage and peanut) or a Sancocho (meat broth with corn, yam, green plantain and toppings). There is something for every taste! In Ecuador, we love to put toppings on our soups, so don't be surprised if you see people putting some popcorn on their tomato soup or some fried bananas on a ceviche. Personally, one of my favourite soups for a winter day is a warm Sancocho. This soup is rich and comforting and it is made on a base of green plantain, yuca (yam), any type of meat broth (you can also make a vegetarian version), a floating piece of corn, and toppings such as freshly chopped coriander, peanut paste, and pickled red onion. Sancocho is a soup that you will find across all the Latin American region in different variations, and this shows that its tradition probably came from Spain. Some people say this soup is similar to certain Spanish dishes such as El Cocido Español and La Olla Criolla.

So where can you find this hearty delicacy? I'd suggest visiting the markets. Just spot the stands that have massive casseroles and the fresh smell of coriander, plantain and corn.

15. UPHOLDING ECUADORIAN GASTRONOMY.

While I was a student of Culinary Arts in Ecuador, I often heard chefs emphasizing that Ecuadorian cuisine had not yet succeeded in becoming international. Many chefs are very proud of cooking local food but still feel that it hasn't reached the goal of becoming its "own brand" in the eyes of the global restaurant industry. Even though there are still no Michelin Star restaurants in the country, there are amazing chefs who attempt to break boundaries with their cooking and challenge tradition through the exploration of the versatility of our local ingredients. In the high-end of local gastronomy, restaurants such as URKO Cocina Local, Quitu, Marcando el Camino, De la Llama, La Purísima, and ZFood Pescadería should be on your list. There are also plenty of low-budget and tasty options such as El Palacio de la Fritada, Empanadas de Morocho Ulloa, Corvinas ¡Don Jimmy! and Cafeteria Modelo in the

Historical Center. More important than a Michelin-Star, is the amount of hungry mouths these restaurant feed and how happy they leave the restaurant after their meal.

16. STREET FOOD IS THE GASTRONOMIC SOUL OF EVERY CITY.

Every city around the world has its own culture of street food. It is through it that we can discover some of the most authentic and often hidden flavours of local gastronomy. Street food in Quito gathers around places where people congregate and where there is a dense human flow. These places can be, for example, outside universities, the mercados ambulantes or informal markets, the parks on the weekend, and the clubs and discotheques at night. If you happen to walk around Universidad Politécnica, also called by its students as "La Poli", you have to visit the Poliburger stands. Here you will find an epic hamburger with an outrageous amount of sauce, cheese and of course, flavour. If you are on a diet, please don't eat it this.

Politécnica is part of a university cluster; so not to far away is Universidad Católica, also known as "La Cato". After class, you will see tons of students gathering around the Cevichocho stands to eat fresh and vegetarian ceviche made of our local bean, the Chocho. There is also a stand of great Corviche down the street, where you can find flavorful patties made of peanut paste, green banana, achiote and a filling of fish. A typical snack from the province of Manabí! Finding street food in Quito is not a hard task, then again, be sure your stomach is feeling confident enough, as these snacks can often be very oily and a little bit heavy on your gut. If you want to take your street food experience to another level, you must eat at D' La Calle, an exciting and contemporary perspective on the concept of street food, proposed by its chef and owner Rafael Mora. This is a stand where you'll find Cocina de Autor at an accessible price and with an urban twist!

17. THE BOOM OF CRAFT BEER.

Pilsener is one of the most truly Ecuadorian beers you will find in the country. It is straightforward, unpretentious, and its taste is simple and fresh. Whether you are in a football match, at the beach or attending a barbecue with friends, you will see it everywhere. You might also enjoy drinking Club, which is slightly more expensive but perfect for every occasion. These two brands of beer have been around since I can remember, and it is just during the last two decades when we started hearing about the concept: Cerveza Artesanal. In Quito, craft beer began as a trend when many young entrepreneurs started noticing the lack of variety in the local beer market and began to experiment with new types of local hops. Their work has been fruitful, and today you can find a big number of craft beer breweries all around Quito. Breweries such as Andes Brewing, Bandido Brewing, Sabai, and Abysmo are some of beer labs and bars where you can have a glass of fresh beer and maybe a pizza, why not? Whether you wish to have a heavenly experience drinking your beer, or are just curious to see what cerveza artesanal is all about, it is worth visiting these various small pubs around the city. The interesting thing about this trend is that it has reactivated nightlife in Quito in a new way and has opened new opportunities for Quiteños to enjoy the nights, by drinking a good glass of beer and having a nice and casual meal with it. Bars such as Café Roscón and L'Abadía in the neighbourhood of La Vicentina are some of the spots where Quiteños eat, drink, and dance during their Friday nights. Just beware, craft beer has a higher alcoholic degree, so having something in your stomach before you drink it is important!

18. CHICHA IS HOW WE ROLL.

Forget about the beer! Who cares about the wine! Ecuador is all about its Chicha.

Chicha de Jora also is known as "corn-beer" is a fermented alcoholic beverage from the Andean and Amazonian regions of Latin America. Its preparation and use date back from pre-hispanic times when the Inca Empire used it as a ceremonial beverage. Today, Chicha has become re-popularized in bars and restaurants around the country, and there are some bars that do a great job in making it. The bar and restaurant Sereno Moreno, located in the neighbourhood of La Tola in Quito, is one of the places where you can taste some amazing homemade Chicha. Sereno Moreno's owner, Josué, has put an amazing amount of effort and creativity in serving one of the best Chicha's in town and also developing other flavours from several different roots. Last time I was there, I tasted Beetroot Chicha, and it was sweet, refreshing and delicious.

19. ACHACHAY, IT'S COLD! BRING CANELAZO!

I admit I am being redundant here, but please remember, Quito can be VERY COLD in winter! Having made this clear, there is a magic beverage Quiteños drink during cold and foggy nights to keep their hearts warm. Canelazo is a warm alcoholic drink made of cinnamon, naranjilla (one of our local fruits), aguardiente, and sugar. It is popular during Fiestas de Quito on a party bus, but it can also be a nice drink to share in a relaxed night with friends. Canelazo is a drink that you will find in almost any bar in the city;

nevertheless, I prefer to drink mine in Guápulo, a lovely and bohemian neighbourhood of the city that emerges from a cliff and looks out to the eastern mountain range of the city.

20. BLUE BIRD.

Hard liquor can be popular in the highlands because it keeps people warm. Blue Bird or Pájaro Azul, on the other hand, is a little bit more special as a drink because of what it contains. Pájaro Azul is an inter-Andean type of aguardiente, originally from the province of Bolívar. It is strong and aromatic, and when you put it against the light you'll see a delicate blue colour come through the glass. No colorants added. Pájaro Azul is made of sugar cane, orange leaves, clementine, chicken meat and anis. Wait a minute, did you say chicken meat? Well yes, I'm not kidding. The chicken is an essential ingredient in this drink. This ancestral beverage is very commonly served during the Fiestas de Guaranda and the carnival celebrations in the province of Bolívar. Nowadays, Pájaro Azúl is sort of a cult drink served all around the country, and if you get the chance you

should definitely try it! Remember you only live
once, or as we say in Ecuador, chulla vida!

21. ECUADORIAN FOOD IS QUITE MEAT-BASED. WHAT IF I AM VEGETARIAN?

Good question. Indeed, Ecuadorian dishes often include meat, and this becomes the most important part of the meal. As I have become mostly vegetarian in the past few years, I've been in my own quest of trying to find the best vegetarian restaurants in Quito and guess what, there are tons of them. In Quito, there are many restaurants that sell fresh lunch for a good price during weekdays, and any of them will offer great vegetarian options. In the cute and bohemian neighbourhood of La Floresta, several restaurants such as Warmi and Buhmi, offer healthy home food with great taste and accessible prices (though slightly more expensive than the typical street food). While Warmi offers both a standard and vegetarian lunch menu, Buhmi's philosophy is to serve only vegan food. Both of them also sell homemade jams, sauces and chutneys to take home, which are simply delicious.

22. OK, THERE IS GREAT FOOD IN QUITO, HOW DO I PAY FOR IT?

In Quito, most restaurants accept credit and debit cards; nevertheless, if you want to get some street snacks on the go or visit some Huecas and markets, it is better to carry around some cash. This is also advisable if you are travelling through the city using public transportation, as all the buses, taxis and trams accept only cash. As transport is so cheap in Ecuador, don't forget to bring your sueltos or coins to avoid frustration as the drivers often don't have change.

23. ANOTHER TRICKY QUESTION: HOW MUCH WILL I PAY FOR MY FOOD?

A bit more than you might expect. As opposed to what many people might tell you about the price of food in Latin America, I wouldn't say eating in Ecuador is necessarily cheap. Of course, this depends on your own notion of what is cheap and what is expensive, but the reality is that the food in supermarkets and average dishes in restaurants tends to be high. The reason for this is that the taxes for imported products have gone up the roof, therefore, most restaurants have a high production cost in their kitchens. Luckily for you, if you want to save money and eat on a budget, the Huecas and markets are normally cheap and offer great food. Restaurants, on the other hand, have higher prices, and a tip is normally expected.

24. AMBATO IS THE LAND OF FRUITS AND FLOWERS.

So you've seen enough of Quito? Maybe we go on a road trip to the South. Ambato, also known as the land of fruits and flowers, is a small Andean city located two hours drive away from the capital. I have a close relationship with this city since my grandmother was born there. She left at a young age due to an earthquake that hit the city in 1949;

nevertheless, a big part of our family still lives there. Ambato is a town that has particularly great food markets on the weekends and people are very dedicated to protect and promote its local dishes. Plato Ambateño is one of the typical dishes of this town. It consists of a fried egg, a generous portion of fritada (slow-cooked pork with beer and garlic), a long stripe of chorizo ambateño (sausage), a spoon of mote (corn) and some encurtido or salad. Ambato is also famous for its baking tradition and offers a diversity of breads such as Pan Ambateño, Pinllo, and Pan de Atocha, which is made with pork fat. These edible jewels from the bakery go perfectly with a good cup of coffee for supper. Ambato, the land of fruits and flowers, is also an important focus of culinary traditions, so if you have a day or two to get out of the capital, don't miss it.

25. HOLY WATER BATHS.

Considering you are still in Ambato eating some chorizo ambateño, maybe you want to take a refreshing bath in the hot springs of its neighbouring town, Baños de Agua Santa, or Baños, in short. This

Eat Like a Local

small city is known as the "gateway to the Amazon" as it is still located in the mountain region but is very near to the jungle. Overlooked by the currently active volcano Tungurahua, this city is surrounded by hundreds of waterfalls and enjoys a warm and humid microclimate. Baños has similar gastronomy to the rest of the highlands, but it is especially known for its sugar cane sweets and juices. Melcocha is their local sweet, a unique clementine and sugar candy made with a special technique. When you walk around town you'll see countless people stretching melted sugar from a pole and looping it over and over again until it has a thick consistency. Well, that is Melcocha, a chewy, sticky and aromatic piece of lovely Baños. Speaking about sugar cane, this town is renown for making the best sugar cane juice in the country, and you can find it in every restaurant or market. Baños is a special place, and if you imagine yourself hiking around waterfalls, bathing in volcanic hot springs and enjoying the city's active nightlife, this place is for you.

26. CRAFT MARKETS IN OTAVALO.

There are towns that are a must-see in all the guides you will ever read about Ecuador. Otavalo is one of them. This lakeside town is known because of its craft markets in the weekend and because of its thriving commerce and tourism. In Otavalo lives a majority of indigenous people from communities of the North of the country. Overlooked by the Imbabura volcano, this cosy town is a perfect destination to find presents to take to loved ones and get a taste of the local culture. If you are visiting Otavalo during September, the festivity of Yamor is taking place and the food assortment served for this celebration, is delightful. This celebration is an act of giving thanks for the second solstice and the season of harvest. Chicha made from the best corn is one of the gifts offered to the Sun. So during Yamor, you can expect to drink abundant Chicha from different types of corn, and accompany it with a huge plate of empanadas, potato tortillas, mote (white corn) and Ají.

Eat Like a Local

27. COTOPAXI VOLCANO: THE NECK OF THE MOON.

Cotopaxi rises over the Andes at an altitude of 5,897 m above sea level. It has erupted more than fifty times since 1738, and its surroundings have been shaped into enormous valleys formed by mudflows and lava rivers. The area around the volcano seems almost extraterrestrial, nevertheless, it hosts an amazing amount of animals such as wild horses, deers, rabbits and Andean foxes. Reaching the summit of Cotopaxi is among the goals of many mountain climbers who visit Ecuador, and if you wish to do it, there are guides who will take you through all the necessary steps to make it happen. If that is not necessarily your dream but you still wish to do a shorter hike, you can climb 500m to its first refuge. No special equipment needed, just a good pair of lungs. The refuge offers climbers a warm cup of hot chocolate or some Coca tea for the altitude sickness. Keep in mind it is more enjoyable to visit this volcano if you have already acclimatised and you feel your body is ready to push its limits a bit higher. If you wish to contemplate the volcano from the bottom and enjoy the view with a good meal, Hosteria

Tambopaxi offers affordable daily meals that will give you the energy to endure the mountain weather. A good Locro with cheese and avocado and a warm Canelazo are on the menu! Tambopaxi also offers accommodation for the night, in case you want to witness a unique sunrise with a unique view of Cotopaxi in the morning!

28. THE AVENUE OF THE VOLCANOES.

The Avenue of the Volcanoes, La Avenida de los Volcanes in Spanish, is a 200 km track where there are as many as seventy-two volcanoes, eighteen of them currently active. If you're feeling adventurous and own a drivers licence, you could make a road trip from Quito to the cultural capital of the country, Cuenca. It takes around ten hours to make this trip by car and it allows you to make a gastronomic tour through the small towns of the Andes. Assuming you left Quito early in the morning, why don't you grab some breakfast at El Café de La Vaca, located near the town of Machachi. Here you can eat a fresh and generous meal made exclusively

Eat Like a Local

with products from the farm. This restaurant also produces its own cheese and milk, and serves traditional snacks such as habas con queso (fava beans with cheese), and mote con chicharron (corn with pork rind). I guess you're full now and can drive a little longer? Let's go! Once you arrive at the city of Latacunga, try to find some Chugchucaras. This traditional and huge dish is a platter of mixed delicacies from the highlands. It includes pork, potatoes, green plantain, empanadas, popcorn and fried pork skin. This dish is quite something. In the rare case you'd still have space in your stomach for some dessert, you should stop at the town of Salcedo, renown for making the best ice-cream in the country. Their avocado ice-cream is superb, and you can find it in any of the dozen of ice-cream shops in town. Try the local specialities of each of these towns, unique culinary traditions worthy of being discovered. As you approach Cuenca, don't forget to stop to see the Inca ruins of Ingapirca, located in the province of Cañar. The flavourful landscapes you will taste throughout this journey will not disappoint you!

29. CUENCA: A CULTURAL AND GASTRONOMIC GEM.

Cuenca, also known as "The Athens of Ecuador" is the culture capital of the country. It does not only have stunning colonial architecture, art biennales, theatres and galleries, but also amazing food. Similarly to many other Andean cities, corn is a very important ingredient in the making of its local dishes. From Tamales and Rosero to Mote-Pata (corn served in veal broth with sausage, bacon, milk and onion), the food in this city has a character of its own. The best traditional comida cuencana can be found in the Huecas located in the neighbourhood Las Herrerías. This long street is vibrant with smells and flavours and it is a great place to eat a fresh Tamal with a cup of coffee. Don't forget to bring cash!

Surrounded by rivers and willows, Cuenca hosts a vibrant scene of restaurants; however, there is one that should be on the top of your list. Tiestos Café is a legendary restaurant in Cuenca because it offers a type of cooking which is hard to find anywhere else. All their dishes are prepared in clay pots (traditionally known as tiestos) and keep inside treasures of taste in the form of stews. Each tiesto is sided by an amazing variety of local pickles and condiments you can dip your bread into. It will be an unforgettable experience for your taste buds. On the other hand, If you wish to eat less meat and more vegetables, you should visit Café Libre, a fresh culinary proposal that offers very intelligent and exquisite vegan cuisine. Forest mushrooms macerated in black tea, beetroot quinoto, avocado in amaranth crust, and pickled red onions, are just some of the local, organic and fresh delicacies offered in its menu.

30. RESERVA NATURAL EL CAJAS: A GIFT FROM THE ICE AGE.

Cuenca is only half an hour away by car to one of the most amazing natural reserves of the country called, El Parque Nacional Cajas. This national park lies over what used to be an Ice Age glacier. Today it offers more than one thousand bodies of water in the shape of lakes. El Cajas ecosystem, known as páramo, is shaped by altitude, humidity and its geographical location, which allows a very specific type of vegetation to exist. Polylepis trees, yellow quinoa, orchids, and different types of moss grow between the lakes. Trouts have been introduced in its waters, therefore after a walk through the park, you can enjoy a fresh piece of fish with fried yam and rice in the national park's cosy café. The restaurant is lovely and outlooks the delicate and fragile landscape made of water and rock. If you wish to stay for a hiking holiday in El Cajas, the Dos Chorreras lodge can host you in its lovely wooden cottages with chimneys. The food is great. They serve nice varieties of local dishes, nevertheless, they are famous for their delightful grilled trout in garlic sauce with shrimps. For dessert, maybe some rice milk with cinnamon will accompany a good coffee.

31. ENJOYING A MEAL IN THE CLOUDY FOREST.

You have now visited the main sites in the Andes and maybe you are curious about what lies beyond the mountains, in the lowlands. In Ecuador, what we call The Cloudy Forest or El Bosque Nublado, is a microclimate where the fog places itself on the tree canopies, covering the whole roof of the

Eat Like a Local

forest and keeping its humidity. This type of climate sustains a huge diversity of flora and fauna. The natural reserve of Maquipucuna, located in the northwest of Quito, protects about 14,000 hectares of forest and therefore 4% of the planet's bird population. Maquipucuna Ecolodge offers accommodation and daily hikes and activities in the reserve. What better place to eat some local delicacies than being surrounded by dozens of birds, butterflies and stunning nature? If you get hungry, you can relax in their lovely restaurant and indulge in their delicious daily homemade meals. From yam patties with Tilapia (the local fish of the region) to Quimbolitos (sweet corn Tamal), the cuisine here is simply heartwarming. They also serve a delicious Babaco Flambee (a sweet compote cooked with the local fruit, babaco) which is lovely. After your meal, why not drinking some fresh coffee produced in the reserve? The Cloudy Forest is renown for its great coffee and cacao production, so if you want to taste them from the source, this is the place to do it.

32. HOW ABOUT SOME WORMS?

Yes, I said WORMS and it was not a typo! The gastronomy of the Ecuadorian Amazon uses local ingredients that might seem unusual to us, but are worth trying! You've travelled from so far anyway, you might as well embrace the adventure. If you visit the province of Pastaza, what about tasting some of their local specialities? Whether you've tried insects in the past or not, this is a great opportunity to taste some big and tasty chontacuros! This type of worms grows in the heart of Chonta trees after being deposited there by black beetles. After a few months, the worms become big and are harvested. They are known for their high caloric content and curative properties. People often prepare them on top of a hot grill, fried in a pan, covered inside a leaf of Bijao or eat them raw with salt. You can find Chontacuros in the town of El Puyo, where the restaurant Napurak has a reputation for preparing delicious grilled worms on wood.

After all, worms are the food of the future!

Eat Like a Local

33. EATING FROM THE RAINFOREST.

Cooking and eating habits in the Ecuadorian Amazon are known for using only the available products from hunting, fishing and harvesting. This type of cuisine tends to be simple, yet extremely fresh and refined. The Amazon is huge, therefore dishes vary from town to town, nevertheless, you will notice it is not rare to find various meals that include alligator, monkey and guanta, a beaver-like mammal of the region. Fish is also widely used and prepared in the form of soups or grilled on charcoal. Yuca or yam is an important root in the regional diet, as Chicha is prepared from it. Personally, one of my favourite dishes from the Amazon is Maito de Pescado. It consists of a piece of fish which is macerated with local spices, wrapped in leaves from a plant known as Bijao, and put on the grill until it's cooked. This juicy and delicate dish is often sided with a good portion of cooked yam and plantain. If you prefer eating a vegetarian meal you can also find mushroom ceviche and palm heart ceviche in abundance. Dishes from the Amazon are known for being highly nutritious and protein-based. In the bigger cities of

Ecuador, people are more and more interested to learn about the ways people cook in this region of the country and are inspired to pursue a type of cuisine that is closer to nature.

34. THE RED SEED.

Whether you are travelling through the Amazon, the Andes, the coast, the North or the South of Ecuador, you will notice a secret ingredient spreading its red colour among all types of dishes: Achiote. This ancestral seed has existed in the American continent for around 5000 years and we use it to colour our typical dishes like Llapingachos, Locro, and Encocado. We also love the slightly nutty, spicy and sweet aroma it adds to our cuisine. Besides its use on food, Achiote has been traditionally used as a body pigment in ethnic groups like the Tsáchilas. The men of the community apply the pigment on their hair and argue that the reason they started doing this is that a wizard suggested that if they'd apply it generously on their body, they would prevent Smallpox. This wizard was right about something, Achiote does have a lot of curative benefits and is a seed with anti-inflammatory properties. It is also used to close small wounds on the skin. Achiote can't really be used raw, but it must be infused into oil in order to extract its colour and properties. This seed is available in any supermarket in different cities.

35. CACAO IS OUR GOLD.

Yes, Cacao is our gold. It has been used not only by the pre-hispanic cultures as a valuable mean of exchange but nowadays it is one of our main products for exportation. Maybe you have tasted Ecuadorian chocolate, but have you ever tasted Cacao fruit? Cacao is an elongated fruit which has a sweet and acid pulp inside, covering its seeds. I'd say the taste resembles the one of passion fruit but with a sweet note. You can find Cacao fruit in market halls, but maybe you want to learn more about where Cacao grows and how it is transformed into chocolate bars. If this is the case, you should make a visit to the local Cacao producers in different regions of the country, including the Galapagos Islands. Ecuadorian chocolate brands such as Pacari, Caoni and Hoja Verde don't only offer amazing bars of chocolate but also place a big emphasis on producing Cacao in a sustainable, organic and environmentally conscious way. Hoja Verde, for example, finds it very important to have traceability of labour from bean to bar and believes that the national chocolate industry can help many families gain quality of life by working in the production of this edible jewel. If you wish to taste local Cacao and watch the whole process of the production yourself, there are several tours that organize visits to the production sites.

I personally love a cup of hot cocoa, and this is my favourite way of consuming Ecuadorian chocolate. You can get a great cup of Pacari hot chocolate in their cafeteria located by La Plaza Grande, in the historical centre of Quito.

36. COFFEE IS ALSO OUR GOLD!

Even though most of my life I have considered myself to be a tea person, when I moved abroad I really started to appreciate the local production of Ecuadorian coffee. When I had the best cup of coffee I have ever had, I didn't expect it. I was in Berlin, and my stepfather had sent me and my boyfriend a bag of coffee beans produced and toasted in the Galapagos Islands. I had never tasted anything like that. This coffee is produced by Café Vélez, a small coffee company that started working in 2007 and focuses on exporting great quality coffee and also ensures fairness of labour. In Ecuador, coffee is grown in hilly terrains found in regions such as Loja, Imbabura, Pichincha, Zamora and Galápagos. However, there is one city in Ecuador where the culture of coffee is especially dominant, and if you are a coffee lover and want to find the best beans, this is a place you must visit!

Zaruma, located in the province of El Oro, is a lovely town with an impressive nineteenth-century, Republican-era architecture that will offer you one of the best cups of coffee in the country. Many people call Zaruma a paradise between the highlands and the coast. Others know it for its gold-mines and banana plantations. Whatever is the reason you end up visiting this lovely town, you might be wondering, where can I get a good cup of coffee? The local people or Zarumeños, recommend Tertulia café, as one of their favourite places to drink coffee. They also recommend Pantera, a traditional cafeteria where you can accompany your cup with some local dishes such as Tigrillo (scrambled eggs with green banana) or a Bolón de Verde (green banana patties filled with cheese or pork meat).

37. COOKING WITH LEAVES.

Remember we talked about Tamales and Humitas? And how these were wrapped inside leaves and then steamed? In Ecuador, no matter the region, people often use different types of leaves as part of their traditional cooking techniques. Corn, Achira, Banana and Bejuco are an essential part of many recipes, and there is a reason for this. The use of leaves doesn't only allow the making of puddings and concentration of flavours in stews, but it also adds a unique and wonderful aroma to each dish. So next time you eat a Tamal Lojano, a Quimbolito, a Tonga or a Maito de Pescado, remember to open your taste buds and pay attention to that special aroma from the leaf.

Eat Like a Local

38. COOKING WITH MUD.

Ecuadorian cuisine is highly creative and resourceful. Ancestral traditions didn't only teach us how to cook with the use of leaves but also with the use of soil itself. In the Andes and coastal regions, it is possible to find a type of cooking known as cocina al barro or "mud cooking". It consists of wrapping any type of protein such as chicken, pork or fish in banana leaves and then covering it with a layer of black mud that comes especially from the Amazon. The dish is then placed in a wood oven until it's ready and then opened with a small hammer to release its tasty insides. Some call it an edible piñata and some others a magic casserole, either way, this is one of many cooking secrets that remind us how much of our pre-hispanic roots are still present in the cooking techniques of today. This culinary wisdom was formulated by the Valdivia Culture, which settled in the coasts of Ecuador around 4,000 B.C. Part of the intangible cultural heritage they left behind is their culinary techniques, which show us the ways they related to nature, to food, and teach us so much about the way they lived when the world was completely different from today. The restaurant Pollo al Barro in

Quito is one of the few restaurants that nowadays cooks with this particular technique, so don't forget to pay them a visit!

39. CEVICHE IS LIFE!

Ceviche is one of our favourite local dishes! It is not only fresh and extremely tasty but it is also a lifesaver when it comes to a hangover, or what we call chuchaqui. Ecuadorian ceviche is different from its cousin, the Peruvian ceviche, and from other Latin American versions. People make Ceviche around the country, using what is available in their region, and adding a different touch to this delicious dish. Ceviche in Ecuador can be made with fish, clams, shrimp, crab, lobster, sea urchin, scallop, etc. These are then mixed with lime juice, bitter orange, grated tomato, fresh red onion, some mustard and ketchup. Oh, and yes, we top our Ceviche with popcorn, plantain chips and tostado (fried corn). From all the Ecuadorian dishes, I must say, one of the most intriguing and even confusing aspects of our gastronomy is putting popcorn on our soups. Why would we do that? I don't really know, but it tastes

Eat Like a Local

great! The best way to taste Ecuadorian ceviche is to travel around the country and taste it from food carts, Huecas and restaurants in each town. Maybe you are brave enough to try a Volquetero, a ceviche that is huge because it combines ingredients from three provinces of the country. You can find this ceviche in El Tena, where it was invented to honour the volqueteros or truck drivers that built the roads in the Amazon.

40. WELCOME TO MANABÍ! READY TO EAT?

Between you and me, this is my favourite type of cuisine in the whole of Ecuador. Manabí is a fantastic province where to eat. This is an opinion shared by many, therefore, its gastronomy was recently declared Immaterial Heritage of Ecuador by the National Institute of Cultural Heritage. When you visit, don't be surprised to see peanut in all your dishes. This is one of the essential ingredients of the famous Cocina Manabita. Some of the typical dishes you should try are Viche de Pescado (fish stew with, peanut, and yuca), Encocado de Langostino (shrimp with coconut milk, pepper and achiote), and some Salprieta (a powdered mixture of salt, peanut and coriander meant to be eaten on top of grilled banana).

The food in this region is a reflection of its people, their strong character, effervescence, and creativity. So where to start in Manabí? I'd suggest you begin your culinary journey in the beautiful town of Puerto López. This small fishing village is part of Machalilla National Park, and it is known for hosting an amazing amount of humpback whales during the months of June to October, season when they come to mate in the equator. This town is also remarkable for it amazing beaches such as Los Frailes, its neighbouring island Isla de la Pata, and the ancestral rich history of the community of Salango. The food in Puerto López is excellent, and all along the coast you will find cobachas or huts built as restaurants, each with its own special flavor. If you are hungry after long hours walking along the colossal coast, you should treat yourself with a Cazuela Manabita. This thick and rich stew is cooked with green banana, onion, fish, shrimp, peanuts and then cooked inside a clay pot. Enjoy it with a good portion of rice, slices of lime and of course, some Ají! Tonga, is another culinary delicacy you can't miss. This ancestral dish from the region includes rice, bananas, and chicken covered in peanut sauce and wrapped in a banana leaf. There are countless of other edible treasures in this region that are worth to be discovered, and each town offers its own seasoning and character to its food!

41. A GUSTATIVE RE-BIRTH.

When you arrive in Ecuador there will be certain places that you will want to say "this is my favourite place". For me, Cocosolo Eco-lodge is my favourite place to eat in Manabí. Located besides Cojimies, a small fisher town surrounded by mangroves and monkey forests, Cocosolo is a hotel and restaurant that borders the ocean and is immersed in a forest of coconut trees. Rustic, eclectic, and relaxed, this eco-lodge is a family business that has existed for over sixty years and wishes to attract visitors who love nature and look for simplicity and rest. The love for cooking is transmitted by the chef and owner Valentina Álvarez through all her dishes. For an Ecuadorian like me, to try her cooking and her re-interpretation of local cuisine was in a way a gustative re-birth. Her cooking, beyond reading recipes and plating them in a creative way, is a deep reflection upon finding the real purpose of the ingredients she uses. From her Pescado al Ajillo (fish confit in garlic) to her Coconut Flan, Valentina's food is the most exciting type of cuisine I can think of. Furthermore, this restaurant will only serve you fish and seafood that is seasonal and will not serve products that are in one way or another degrading the fragile environment of Cojimies.

42. THE THREE KINDS OF MILK OF THE COCONUT.

This chapter I am going to continue rambling about Cocosolo, so please bear with me for the next few lines. Remember when I told you it is a hidden gem in a huge plantation of coconut trees? Well, now you know where all those coconuts go. One of the reasons this restaurant is great is because they created their own DIY technology to process ingredients. One of the tools they have made is a coconut press that extracts the "three types of milk of the coconut": coconut water, coconut milk, and coconut cream. No wonder their langoustine encocado is mind-blowing. Their innovation in taste and in cooking tools take their cuisine to a new level that is hard to find anywhere else in Ecuador.

43. G-KILL CITY. THE HOME OF THE BEST ENCEBOLLADO.

Guayaquil, or as their residents call it G-Kill City, is a riverside metropolis of contrasts. From its food and to its people, this city offers a unique intensity and wildness hardly seen anywhere else in the country. Guayaquil is one of the biggest cities in Ecuador and besides being known for being the economic pole of the country, it is also renown for its great gastronomy. This city is the motherland of one of my favourite fish soups: Encebollado. This dish is made with Albacora fish, yuca (yam), onions, tomato, pepper, chilli and herbs and it is commonly eaten from late hours in the night to early hours in the morning. Famously known as a "levanta muertos", this soup is praised for its curative faculties after a bad hangover, thus reviving from the dead many partying souls after a long night of dancing. It is said that Encebollado has its origins in the Valdivia culture, where people cooked Albacora in a ceramic casserole with yam on top of wood and fire. With the conquest, the dish changed as people started to add herbs and other ingredients brought by the Spaniards. Some of the best places where you can get your Encebollado are La Picantería D' Danilo, where this soup has been prepared for the past thirty-eight years; or Cevicheria Rosita, located at El Antiguo Mercado Sur.

44. THE GALAPAGOS ISLANDS: WHERE TO EAT ON A FRAGILE PARADISE?

The Galapagos Islands, also known as The Enchanted Islands are the fourth region of Ecuador or as we call it "la región insular". The archipelago is one of the most precious natural reserves in the world, and when Spanish sailors first spotted it in the 1500's they couldn't believe they were real. A "mirage", they called them while observing their hills immersed in the mist. The Galapagos Islands have been part of countless myths, been site of shipwrecks, hosted pirates, and later became Charles Darwin's living laboratory and the home of lonely George. These

Eat Like a Local

islands are indeed enchanted, as they sustain flora and fauna that doesn't exist anywhere else in the world.

The Galapagos are a fragile paradise, so when you visit, be aware that something as basic as your eating habits, might affect negatively certain species of animals and plants. My advice on this subject is concrete. Eat local and support the restaurants and businesses promoted by local chefs. They are the ones who know best what species of fish are not endangered and therefore OK to eat, and when is the closed season for lobster and crab consumption. Depending on what island you are visiting, you will find both delicious and sustainable eating options. On the island of Santa Cruz, for example, you can eat in La Garrapata, which opened some thirty years ago; and until today it serves seafood and fish carefully selected for consumption. It is also famous for preparing a delicate citrus sauce, made with lemons collected from the highlands of the island. Everything on its menu is attentively developed with environmental consciousness. Isla Grill is another eatery known for working with the same philosophy. All the products are local, organic and certified. Here you can even drink Ecuadorian wine! A trip to the Galapagos Islands is a chance for you to witness a unique natural ecosystem while eating well and ecologically. Remember you are very lucky to be able to make this trip, it will be an experience you'll never forget. Then again, don't forget you also have a great responsibility in protecting the precious habitats you will visit!

45. DURING EASTER, WE EAT FANESCA!

There is an essential subject that I still haven't tackled in this guide. What are the biggest festivities in Ecuador and what do Ecuadorians eat to celebrate them? During the next few chapters I will introduce you to some of our biggest culinary traditions related to our local festivities. Let's start with Fanesca. This traditional soup is too good to be ignored. It is eaten for Easter around the country and it exemplifies perfectly the food "mestizaje" that has shaped so many of our traditional recipes. This rich soup generally contains figleaf gourd (sambo), pumpkin (zapallo), and twelve different kinds of beans and grains including chochos (lupines), habas (fava beans), lentils, peas, corn and others. This soup is commonly cooked together with bacalao (salt cod) boiled in milk. Besides its main ingredients and inherent complexity, the soup is then garnished with hard-boiled eggs, fried plantains, herbs, parsley, and empanadas. This dish combines the ancestral tradition of grains in the Andes with the concept of Catholic Easter, brought from Spain. The use of salted cod in the dish is also a culinary tradition imported from the other side of the Atlantic. One of the most remarkable variations of this soup can be found in the Galapagos Islands, where they cook a black Fanesca. I tried it for the first and only time while I was visiting Isla Santa Cruz in 2014. Its black colour comes from the use of black beans, which are found in the Ecuadorian Coast rather than in the Andean region. So if you happen to be visiting Ecuador in April you can't miss this local delicacy!

46. CHRISTMAS IN THE TROPICS. REALLY?

Let me get this straight, if your ideal Christmas holiday is winter land, huskies, reindeers, and winter sports, maybe Ecuador is not the best place for you to visit in this season. While in the highlands it will technically be "winter", this only means that it is the rainy season and that it is still very likely you will be wearing a t-shirt on Christmas day. The coast, on the other hand, will be enjoying of its summer season during December, so just remember to bring your swimming suit and some sunblock. So, what do Ecuadorian families cook for a Christmas in the tropics? Well, it depends on where you are in the country. In Quito, many families prepare baby pork in the oven with spices. This dish is often accompanied by rice with nuts, and a variety of salads. Tamales are also important to have on the table. For dessert, we cook the traditional recipe of rice milk and maybe some pastries with honey, also known as Buñuelos. In Guayaquil, families prepare a good piece of pork leg (pernil) and Manabí's Christmas tables are known for being packed with goodies from the sea. Dishes such as fish with a crab, shrimp and octopus sauce are known to be popular during this time of the year. Anywhere you find yourself spending Christmas, you can find many of these traditional festive meals at the markets. Remember, if you are planning to visit the country this next Christmas, bring your sunglasses!

47. BURNING THE OLD AND BUILDING THE NEW.

So, Christmas is over and you don't want to hear anything even slightly related to food. You have been fed to the extreme and you would need two stomachs to digest all the food you've eaten. Luckily for you, Ecuadorian New Years celebration is not so much about eating, but more about burning the bad and welcoming the new. I love to spend New Year's in Ecuador because of the weirdness and fun it involves. Yeah sure, there is partying and dancing, people screaming numbers backwards too. But what happens before all of this is what is unique. In Ecuador, we have the tradition of building a puppet filled with sawdust, putting a mask on it (normally the face of the president) and then burning it. We call this El Año Viejo, and symbolically it represents the end of the old year and the beginning of the new one. After all, the New Year is about starting from a clean slate, borrón y cuenta nueva. So what do people eat while planning what to burn from the old year and what to save for the next? Most families actually eat the same or similar meal to what they ate in Christmas eve. Many people also eat twelve grapes, when the clock has hit midnight, as a representation of the New Year wishes. Boiled wine and Canelazo are cosy drinks to have in hand while waiting for the old to end and the new to begin!

48. THE DAY OF THE DEAD.

Now that we are talking about meals and festivities in Ecuador, there is another incredibly special season you might pick for your next culinary trip. The Day of the Dead or Día de Los Muertos in Ecuador is a tradition where food and drink are a symbol of remembrance of the dead. Indigenous families have the tradition to visit their deceased loved ones in cemeteries and offer them gifts, meals and music, many of them also stay for a picnic and share some time of reflection and memory with the ones that today are gone. Ecuadorian families in this day also cook two delicacies known as Colada Morada (Spiced berry drink) and Guaguas de Pan (bread figures shaped like babies or dolls). During this ritual, families bake together bread in shapes of "guaguas" (babies in Quechua) and cook a huge casserole of a fruity and thick warm drink. After the baking is done,

Eat Like a Local

we all sit together, dip our guagua into the colada, and enjoy! During these festivities, all the bakeries make and decorate their bread dolls in their own way, pick your favourite one! Also, remember that the best Colada Morada is the one that has abundant pieces of fruit floating inside.

49. I'M TIRED OF ECUADORIAN FOOD, IS THERE SOMETHING ELSE?

What did you just say? You are tired of Ecuadorian food? (sigh) Ok, I guess this time I can swallow my disappointment and give you some tips for the moment when you want to change your flavour palette. In Ecuador as in any other country, you can find a good variety of international cuisine. The question is, which is the best? In Quito, you can find very good Peruvian restaurants, such as Segundo Muelle. Here you can delight your taste buds with some classic Peruvian dishes and their Japanese, Chinese and Spanish influences. Speaking about Chinese, what about a visit to Pekin? Pekin is one of the oldest Chinese restaurants in the capital, and since it opened, the amazing flavours of their Cantonese cooking haven't changed one bit. If the day is hot, and you want to eat something fresh, you can visit the Japanese restaurant Noé. It serves great fresh dishes of Sashimi, made with local fish, and Ecuadorian-Japanese fusion rolls.

50. CHAU ECUADOR! WHAT FLAVOURS WILL I TAKE WITH ME?

Sadly, your time in Ecuador is over! Unless you loved it and decided to stay living here. That wouldn't surprise me! But in the case you are moving towards other horizons, maybe you wish to take some flavourful memories with you. Between these, you should definitely include several varieties of Ecuadorian chocolate, a good bag of coffee, some seeds of achiote so you can colour your future dishes, and if you are travelling not so far, why not taking some frozen Tamales and Humitas? You will miss them! Thank you for joining me through this culinary journey around Ecuador. Now it is up to you to try all these delicacies in carne propia! I hope this guide has given you an insight into our culture, traditions and flavours! Hopefully, this will not be the last time you visit Ecuador, which is as you know by now, more than an imaginary line!

Las hojas saludan al Viento del verano.

En el medio del universo
El sol se reproduce en días.

-Manuel Federico Ponce- Poemas de un Sol Indígena

- - - - - - - - - - - -

OTHER RESOURCES:

LONELY PLANET ECUADOR:https://www.lonelyplanet.com/ecuador

WANDERBUS ECUADOR:
https://www.wanderbusecuador.com/ecuador-guide/

OUGH GUIDES:
https://www.roughguides.com/destinations/south-america/ecuador/

READ OTHER BOOKS BY CZYK PUBLISHING

Greater Than a Tourist- St. Croix US Birgin Islands USA: 50 Travel Tips from a Local by Tracy Birdsall

Greater Than a Tourist- Toulouse France: 50 Travel Tips from a Local by Alix Barnaud

Children's Book: *Charlie the Cavalier Travels the World* by Lisa Rusczyk

Eat Like a Local

Follow *Eat Like a Local* on Amazon.
Join our mailing list for new books
http://bit.ly/EatLikeaLocalbooks

Made in the USA
Monee, IL
03 February 2023

27083920R00059